To...

1 Corinthians 1:3

May God our Father and the Lord Jesus Christ give you grace and peace.

(New Living Translation)

From...

May God Bless you with Peace

May God bless you with peace –
Peace in your heart and peace in your home,
Peace for yourself and peace for your loved ones,
Peace for today's decisions,
Peace for tomorrow's plans,
Peace of mind in all things.
May God's restoring, reassuring peace
surround you always.

Charles Kinsey, Bristol Balloon Fiesta

God's Promise of Peace

Isaiah 54:10

"Though the mountains be shaken
and the hills be removed,
yet my unfailing love for you will not be shaken
nor my covenant of peace be removed,"
says the LORD, who has compassion on you.

(New International Version)

Strive for Peace

Richard Ward, West Pentire Poppies

May our mouths speak words of peace;
May our feet walk in the way of peace;
May our hearts overflow with peace;
May our hands work for peace.
And with God's help, may we always demonstrate
His love and peace in our lives.

•

It isn't enough to talk about peace.
One must believe in it.
And it isn't enough to believe in it.
One must work at it.

Eleanor Roosevelt
Former First Lady of the United States, 1884–1962

If we have no peace, it is because we have forgotten
that we belong to each other.

Mother Teresa
Albanian–Indian Roman Catholic nun and missionary, 1910–1997

Seeking Peace

Sometimes life is so hectic
that we have to consciously stop,
take a moment to ourselves, take a breath,
then pause and pray that God will speak his
peace and wisdom into our lives
to enable us to find 'the missing peace'.

Psalm 46:10

"Be still, and know that I am God!"

(New Living Translation)

No God, no peace.
Know God, know Peace.

Jonathan Leach, Chalkhill Blue Butterfly

Believers, look up –
take courage.
The angels are nearer
than you think.

Billy Graham
American evangelist, 1918–2018

Jonathan Leach, An Autumn Walk

Peace in times of Worry

Our Father God loves us and invites us to hand our anxiety over to him
by turning our worries into prayers.
He wants us to be at peace, not in pieces.

Philippians 4:6–7

Do not be anxious about anything,
but in every situation, by prayer and petition,
with thanksgiving, present your requests to God.
And the peace of God, which transcends
all understanding,
will guard your hearts and your minds in Christ Jesus.

(New International Version)

Peace in times of Conflict

Peace cannot be kept by force;
it can only be achieved by understanding.

Albert Einstein
Theoretical physicist 1879–1955

Always take time to listen to others.
Try to understand their point of view.
Make an effort to explain your own thoughts
quietly, gently, patiently.
Aim for mutual understanding.
Look for points of agreement.
Seek areas of compromise.
Make every effort to put things right.
Endeavour to find a way forward.

Ephesians 4:26

Don't let the sun go down
while you are still angry...

(New Living Translation)

For every minute you remain angry
you give up 60 seconds of peace of mind.

Ralph Waldo Emerson
American essayist and philosopher, 1803–1882

Jonathan Leach, Poppy

Peace in times of Difficulty

Charles Kinsey, Poland

When we put our problems in God's hands,
he puts his peace in our hearts.
Remember, nothing is impossible for God.

John 16:33

"I have told you all this so that
you may have peace in me.
Here on earth you will have many
trials and sorrows.
But take heart, because I have overcome
the world."

(New Living Translation)

Never forget: God is bigger than your problems.
Whatever worries press upon you today,
put them in God's hands and leave them there.

Billy Graham
American evangelist, 1918–2018

Peace in the Storm

One day, a fierce storm blew up when Jesus was in a boat with his disciples. Jesus was fast asleep in the back of the boat, but the disciples were wide awake and terrified, and the boat began to fill with water. When they woke him, Jesus spoke directly to the storm. "Peace; be still!" he said, and the wind and the waves immediately obeyed him.

If Jesus can calm the weather and bring peace to the wind and the waves, how much more can he calm our hearts and bring peace into our situation?

Charles Kinsey, Chanonry Point, Moray Firth

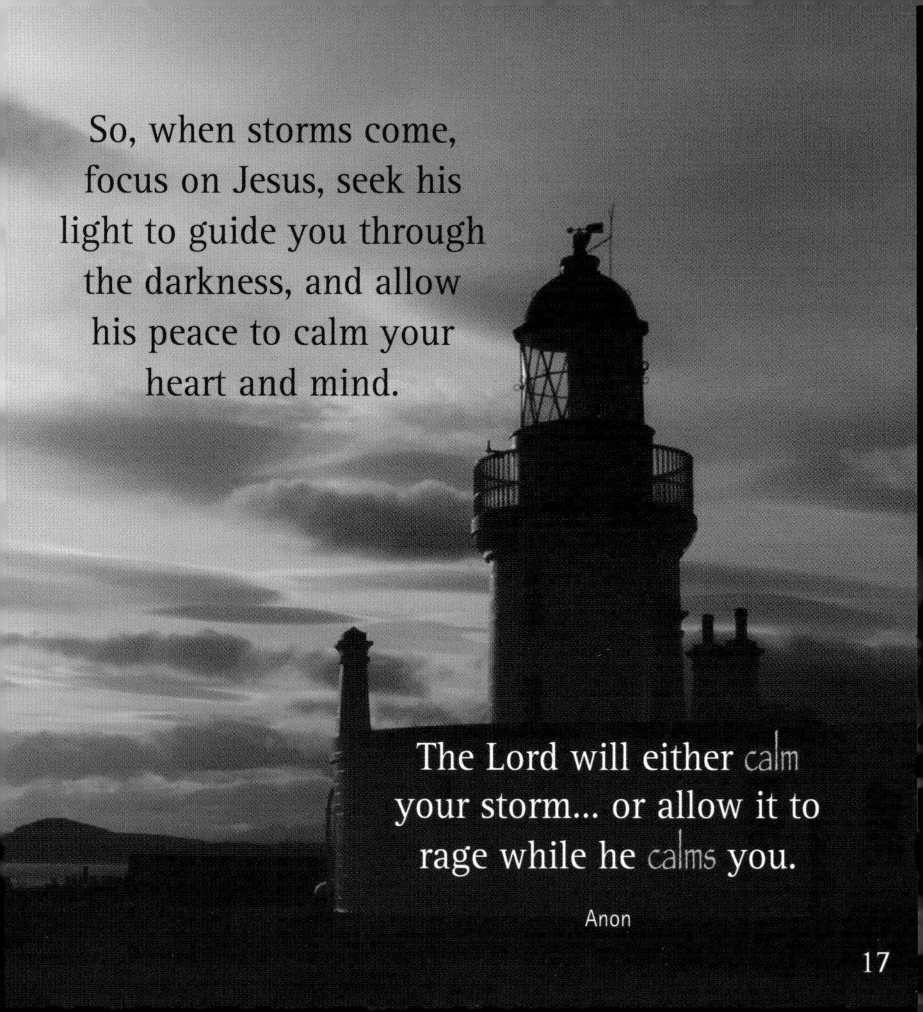

So, when storms come, focus on Jesus, seek his light to guide you through the darkness, and allow his peace to calm your heart and mind.

The Lord will either calm your storm... or allow it to rage while he calms you.

Anon

Perfect Peace

When life is hectic and beset with
problems and complications,
it's good to turn away from our frantic
activity and take time to focus on God.
Perfect peace can be found when
nothing comes between us and God,
and we invite him to direct our path.

In the original Hebrew, the term perfect
peace is actually 'shalom shalom'.
God offers us not just a single portion
of peace, but 'shalom shalom' –
a double serving, a generous helping,
an abundance of peace,
peace that will overflow from us
and spill over to others.

Isaiah 26:3

You will keep in perfect peace
all who trust in you,
all whose thoughts
are fixed on you!

(New Living Translation)

Jonathan Merrell, Whinlatter Forest

Heartfelt Peace

While you are proclaiming peace
with your lips,
be careful to have it even more
fully in your heart.

Saint Francis of Assisi
Italian friar and preacher, 1182–1226

Christ alone can bring lasting peace –
peace with God – peace among
men and nations – and peace
within our hearts.

Billy Graham
American evangelist, 1918–2018

Judith Merrell, Japanese Anemone

Richard Ward, Tulips

Beautiful Silence

Sometimes we are so busy telling God
what we want him to do for us that
we fail to hear his quiet voice speaking to us.
Make time and space for silence and then listen
for God's voice with your heart and mind.

In the silence of the heart, God speaks.
If you face God in prayer and silence,
God will speak to you.

Mother Teresa
Albanian-Indian Roman Catholic nun and missionary, 1910-1997

Go placidly amid the noise and haste,
and remember what peace there may be in silence.

Max Ehrmann
American writer, 1872-1945, taken from his poem, Desiderata

Judith Merrell, Dandelion Clock

Peace and Harmony

Lord, in the quietness reach out and hold me.
Draw me gently into your peace.
And in the loving silence at your heart,
attune my ears to hear the sounds I never listen to.
The harmony that lies in you,
the discords in the world you've put me in.
The laughter and the tears in other people's lives.

...

Above all, may I hear the gentle echoes of your love,
reflected all around me.

Eddie Askew, *Christian writer and artist, 1927–2007*
extract from Breaking the Rules, 1992

Colossians 3:14

Above all, clothe yourselves with love,
which binds us all together in perfect harmony.

(New Living Translation)

Peace and Restoration

Psalm 23:1–3

The LORD is my shepherd; I have all that I need.
He lets me rest in green meadows;
he leads me beside peaceful streams.
He renews my strength.
He guides me along right paths,
bringing honour to his name.

(New Living Translation)

•

Lord, thank you that when we are weary
and worn out, we can find rest in you.
You provide comfort and peace
and restore our hearts and minds.

Jonathan Leach, Spring Lambs

Prince of Peace

Jesus is God's master plan,
His special master-peace,
born to bring peace on earth,
The Prince of PEACE.

Isaiah 9:6

For a child is born to us.
A son is given to us;
and the government will be on his shoulders.
His name will be called
Wonderful Counsellor,
Mighty God,
Everlasting Father,
Prince of Peace.

(World English Bible)

Peace be with you

In some church services the minister might say, 'Let us offer one another a sign of peace'. When we share this peace with one another, we often say the same words that Jesus said when he greeted his disciples after his resurrection, "Peace be with you".

Peace is a gift from God the Father, given to us through the Lord Jesus and, through the power of the Holy Spirit, we can share his peace with others.

Romans 15:33

And now may God, who gives us his peace,
be with you all. Amen.

(New Living Translation)

Judith Merrell, St David's Cathedral

We are God's agents of peace in the world,
He wants us to speak his peace, love and hope
in every situation.

•

Did I offer peace today?
Did I bring a smile to someone's face?
Did I say words of healing?
Did I let go of my anger and resentment?
Did I forgive? Did I love?
These are the real questions.

Henri Nouwen
Dutch Catholic priest and theologian, 1932–1996

Try to keep your soul always in peace and quiet,
always ready for whatever our Lord
may wish to work in you.

Saint Ignatius
Spanish priest and theologian,1491–1556

Jonathan Leach, Wildflower Meadow

Peace and Sanctuary

Everyone needs their own peaceful place,
a refuge from distractions and demands,
a quiet sanctuary, a special place to think and
pray and recover the right perspective on life.
Some find sanctuary in music; others relish the
beautiful outdoors, and some prefer a quiet
corner somewhere special.

Judith Merrell, Over the Waves

We all need to identify our own perfect place of sanctuary, whether it's a ramble through the woods, a stroll along the beach or an armchair by the fire. Everyone finds peace in their own way, and sometimes we need to find it quickly when life closes in.

Lord, help me make a quiet place,
a space where you and I can meet at peace.

Eddie Askew

Christian writer and artist, 1927–2007

Charles Kinsey, Peaceful Lake

Gaelic Blessing

Deep peace of the running waves to you.
Deep peace of the flowing air to you.
Deep peace of the quiet earth to you.
Deep peace of the shining stars to you.
Deep peace of the watching shepherds to you.
Deep peace of the Son of Peace to you.

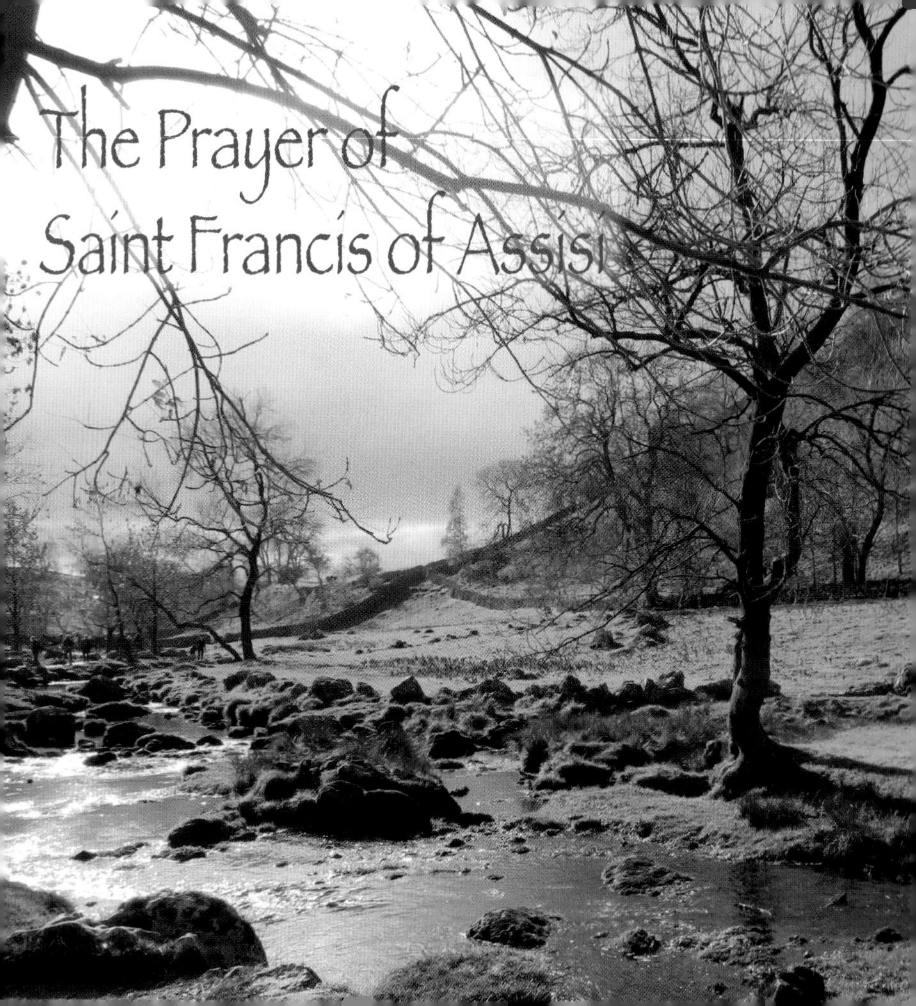

The Prayer of Saint Francis of Assisi

Lord, make me an instrument of your peace.
Where there is hatred, let me sow love;
Where there is injury, pardon;
Where there is doubt, faith;
Where there is despair, hope;
Where there is darkness, light;
And where there is sadness, joy.
O Divine Master,
grant that I may not so much seek
to be consoled as to console;
to be understood as to understand;
to be loved, as to love.
For it is in giving that we receive;
it is in pardoning that we are pardoned;
and it is in dying that we awake to eternal life.

Heather Hulett, Tranquil Waters, Malham

May the Lord support us
all the day long,
till the shades lengthen
and the evening comes,
and the busy world is hushed,
and the fever of life is over,
and our work is done.
Then, in his mercy,
may he give us a safe lodging and a holy rest
and peace at the last.

John Henry Newman
Irish Cardinal, 1801–1890

Richard Ward, Long Shadows

Peace at Night

Jonathan Leach, Otters

At the end of the day,
before you turn out the light,
give all your worries and concerns to God.
Ask Him to calm your mind
and bring peace to your thoughts
so that you may sleep peacefully knowing
that God has got everything in hand.

Psalm 4:8

In peace I will lie down and sleep,
for you alone, O LORD,
will keep me safe.

(New Living Translation)

Go to sleep in peace. God is awake.

Victor Hugo
French writer, 1802–1885

Jonathan Leach, Cherry Blossom